WorDPLay GroUNDHOG
PreseNts

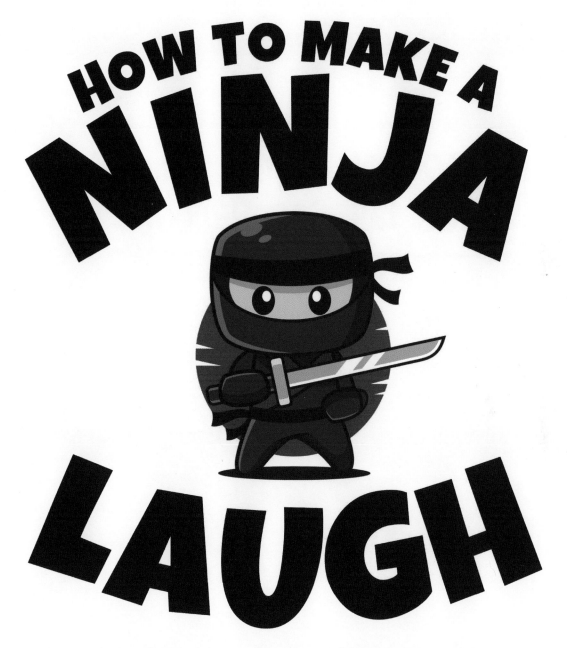

HOW TO MAKE A NINJA LAUGH

A WORDPLAY GROUNDHOG BOOK

More Fun Books By WordPlay Groundhog

HOW TO MAKE AN ASTRONAUT LAUGH

HOW TO MAKE A UNICORN LAUGH

HOW TO MAKE A ROBOT LAUGH

HOW TO MAKE A PENGUIN LAUGH

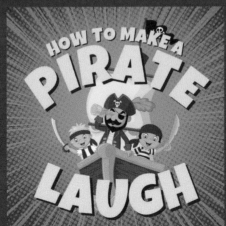

HOW TO MAKE A PIRATE LAUGH

HOW TO MAKE A KOALA LAUGH

WORDPLAYGROUNDHOG.COM

Printed in Great Britain
by Amazon

42518436R00021